Sports Stars

GARY CARTER

The Kid

By Ray Buck

 CHILDRENS PRESS, CHICAGO

Cover photograph: Vic Milton
Inside photographs courtesy of the following:
Nancy Hogue, pages 6, 13, and 32
Ira Golden, pages 8, 10, 11, 15, 25, 27, and 34
Vic Milton, pages 18, 22, and 29
Kevin W. Reece, pages 20 and 37
Steven Jenner, page 39

Library of Congress Cataloging in Publication Data

Buck, Ray, 1947-
    Gary Carter, the Kid.

    (Sport stars)
    Summary: A brief biography of the California-born All-Star
catcher of the Montreal Expos.
    1. Carter, Gary, 1954-   —Juvenile literature.
2. Baseball players—United States—Biography—Juvenile
literature. [1. Carter, Gary, 1954-   . 2. Baseball players.]
I. Title.   II. Series.
GV865.C319B827 1984   796.357′092′4 [B] [92] 83-21084

ISBN 0-516-04337-4

1 2 3 4 5 6 7 8 9 10 11 12 R 91 90 89 88 87 86 85 84

Sports Stars

GARY CARTER

The Kid

Gary Carter is the All-Star catcher of the Montreal Expos. He wears Number 8 on his back and a big smile on his face. They call him The Kid.

The Kid loves life. The Kid loves people. He lets everybody know it in two different languages.

Montreal is the second-largest French-speaking city in the world. The Kid comes from California. Since he loves to talk, he has had to learn a few French words.

Tim Raines, an Expos outfielder, and Gary

The smile is the same in any language.

Receveur d'etoiles is French for all-star catcher. That means Gary Carter. And that means The Kid.

Even his teammates, who are years younger than Gary, call him The Kid.

His corporation is called "Kid 8 Worldwide."

His telephone answering service says, "Hello. Please leave your name and number. The Kid will get back to you."

He even wears "Kid" T-shirts.

"I don't need drugs to make me feel good," Gary says. "I read somewhere that 93 percent of the people in the United States don't enjoy their jobs. I'm one of the lucky ones. I love my job.

Gary gladly signs autographs.

The Kid loves baseball and life.

"I don't feel I'm going out of my way to be nice to people."

Gary Carter has made millions of fans in two countries—the United States and Canada.

You want a Gary Carter autograph? Easy. Just ask him.

All his fan mail is answered personally. Gary says he signs between 100,000 and 200,000 autographs each year.

The Kid explains, "I feel that's part of the game."

It is a game he loves. Gary still collects baseball cards. He has 40,000. If you laid all his baseball cards end to end, they would stretch almost two miles.

"I'm not just a baseball player," he says. "I'm a great fan of the game, too."

Gary's favorite baseball card is one of himself. It shows a handsome 21-year-old rookie catcher swinging a bat. It was Gary Carter's first baseball card of Gary Carter.

The Kid is 29 years old. He and his wife, Sandy, have kids of their own. Christy, 4, wants to be a dancer. Kimberly, 2, is just happy being a toddler. The family pet is a dog named Tina.

The Kid makes a great dad.

"You have to have fun," Gary says. "You have to keep 'the kid' in you." And he does.

Gary talks with the Expos first baseman Al Oliver.

Growing up in Orange County, California, Gary had lots of heroes. His favorite baseball player in the world was Mickey Mantle, Number 7 of the New York Yankees.

"I wore Number 7 in Pony League," says The Kid. "But when I got older, the bigger uniforms always came with the bigger numbers. Those were the uniforms that fit me."

In high school, he played shortstop, third base, and first base. He tried to copy Pete Rose. He learned to hustle all the time.

Gary explains, "I wanted to swing the bat one more time. I wanted to take one more grounder.

I would sprint to my position. I hustled everywhere I went. I wanted to be just like Pete Rose."

Today, Rose is a Gary Carter fan. They are alike in so many ways.

"Like me," Pete says, "Gary thinks he's the best."

There is nothing wrong with *thinking* you're the best. Superstars usually do that. They *think* it, then they go out and *do* it.

Like Pete Rose, Gary Carter probably could have become an all-star at any position. Why did The Kid choose to be a catcher?

Pro scouts told him, "Catching is the quickest way to the big leagues."

It didn't take Gary long to get himself a fat catcher's mitt. He went behind the plate. He tried to look good.

But he was terrible.

"I was the worst catcher in the world when I started out," Gary remembers. "I was timid. I swung my head on every pitch. I threw like I had a football arm. My legs were killing me."

But he would not quit.

Gary learned how to throw quickly. He learned how to throw accurately. He looked around for the best catcher to copy. He picked Johnny Bench. The Kid never ran out of heroes.

His Number 1 hero was always his father.

"My father was my Little League coach," Gary says. "In high school, I was the quarterback. Dad took care of the scoreboard. He was always there for us kids.

"He was my real hero. And he still is."

Gary's mother died of leukemia in 1966. She was only 37 years old. Gary was 12. It was the saddest time of his life.

"I'll always have a place in my heart for anybody who loses a parent." Gary says. "My father became my father and my mother. Sports became my outlet."

So, Gary turned to football and baseball and basketball. He practiced hard. He grew stronger. He kept busy. The Kid was quickly becoming one of a kind.

His best sport was not baseball. His best sport was football.

In fact, Gary became the national champion among seven-year-olds in the first-ever Punt, Pass, & Kick contest in 1961.

He won a trip to the Pro Football Hall of Fame in Canton, Ohio. He was taken on a tour of the White House in Washington, D.C. He even made his first TV commercial for Punt, Pass, & Kick.

"It was really exciting," he says. "That was a great start for me."

Gary nearly won the Punt, Pass, & Kick contest again the following year.

Once again, he got all the way to the national finals. He was proud. He was confident. He was good.

The Kid held a big lead after two events—punting and kicking. That left passing. He usually could throw the ball 40 or 50 yards. There were two finalists in each age group. Each boy was given one chance. And one chance only.

It was a great day for Eskimos. The field was wet and cold. The temperature was 13 degrees. But the wind chill factor was 25 below zero!

Gary thought he was ready—until he slipped.

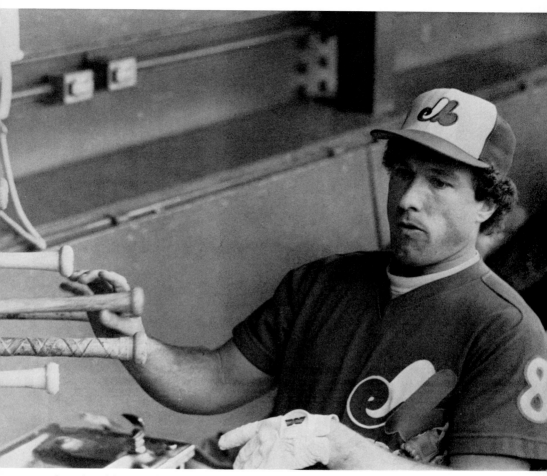

Gary has hit more home runs than any player in the Expos history.

He was wearing tennis shoes. When he went to throw the ball, he nearly landed on his head. The ball landed only 15 feet away.

The Kid lost.

But he learned a lesson that day. Sometimes you try hard and lose, but at least you try. Gary had done the best he could.

"My advice to kids is to work as hard as they can," Gary says. "Don't give up. If they think they have the talent to do something, prove it. Do it."

That's what made Gary Carter a superstar. He played hard. He practiced hard. He studied

hard. The Kid graduated from high school in the top 50 of his class.

Homework was never quite as much fun as tossing around a ball. But grades were still important to Gary. School and sports went together. Gary took neither one for granted.

"I could always find a game to play," he says. "Baseball, basketball, football, you name it. The good Lord blessed me with natural talent. Sports came easy to me.

"But if it doesn't come easy to you, you can still work hard to make yourself better. Practice makes perfect. I think baseball people look for enthusiasm and desire in a player."

When Gary was 12 years old, he was an All-Star pitcher. His record was 13-0. He pitched a couple of no-hitters and one perfect game. He batted .667 with 10 or 12 home runs in 20 games.

His father was the coach. "So, I never got away with anything," Gary laughs.

Football was his best sport. He was a high school All-American twice. He dreamed of going to college. He dreamed of being a star quarterback.

But those dreams were shattered one late summer afternoon in 1971. Gary hurt his right knee. His mind was made up for him.

There would be no football career for The Kid.

Gary was a senior at Sunnyhills High School when it happened. Sunnyhills got together that day with Linwood High for a scrimmage. It was supposed to be just practice.

"We wore our old gray practice stuff," Gary remembers. "Linwood showed up wearing game uniforms. They were serious."

They sure were. On the second play, Gary kept the ball and tried to run around left end.

One Linwood player grabbed him high. Another grabbed him low. They all fell into a 600-pound pile of pain. Gary received all the pain.

Three days later, Gary went to the hospital

Gary studies every hitter in the league.

for a knee operation. He had torn ligaments.

No longer would he have to wonder, "Baseball or football?"

"My decision was made for me that day," Gary says. "I was a baseball player after that."

He has never been sorry about that. He has been a star.

The Montreal Expos will continue paying him about $1.7 million a year until the year 1989. That's when The Kid turns 35 years old.

"I wonder if they'll call me 'Man Carter' by then," he says with a boyish grin.

A catcher's legs are bent like a pretzel.

By 1989, Gary should own a bunch of the major league records for a catcher. Johnny Bench holds most of them now. The Kid wants to catch his hero. Then he can retire.

"I love the game," Gary says. "Maybe I will become a broadcaster someday. I'll just wait and see. Or maybe I'll go into the movies. A few people have told me that I would be pretty good at it."

A catcher must think about his future. The job is painful after awhile. A catcher's legs are always bent like a pretzel.

"I feel it in the mornings," Gary says. "Sometimes it takes me 30 minutes to get out of bed.

There are days when I can't walk down the stairs without popping my legs back into shape."

But The Kid keeps catching. He catches more games every year than anyone else in the National League. He set a record by leading the league in games caught six seasons in a row.

A catcher must have the mind and body of Superman.

He can't let a batting slump bother him. He has to handle the pitchers. He has to give the signals. He is in the driver's seat.

Gary can't let sore legs bother him. He has to bat. He has to catch. It is the most demanding job in baseball.

"I don't want my pitchers to think too much," Gary says. "I study the scouting reports. I learn about every hitter in the league. I know what pitches he can hit and what he can't."

Which ones do you think he calls for?

Gary's older brother, Gordon, was an outfielder in the minor leagues. He played two years in the San Francisco Giants' farm system. Then he quit.

The Kid, meanwhile, has played in six All-Star Games. The fans gave him the most votes of any player in 1982.

Gary is both popular and talented.

He has already won three Gold Gloves in a row for his defense.

He has already hit more home runs than any player in Montreal Expos history.

Now he wants to become the fourth catcher in major-league history to ever hit .300 with 30 home runs and 100 runs-batted-in all in the same season.

He keeps coming close. His legs usually hurt, but you wouldn't know it by the smile on his face.

As he says, "The better you look, the better you play."

The Kid is looking good.

CHRONOLOGY

1954 —Gary Edmund Carter is born on April 8.

1961 —Gary wins the first national Punt, Pass, & Kick contest for seven year olds.

1962 —Gary is the national Punt, Pass, & Kick runner-up for eight year olds.

1966 —At the age of 12, Gary is an All-Star pitcher on his father's team.

1972 —The Montreal Expos pick Gary in the third round of the 1972 free-agent draft.

1974 —Gary plays his first major league games in September. His first home run comes off Steve Carlton.

1975

Feb. —Gary marries Sunnyhills High Homecoming Queen Sandy Lahm.

Oct. —*The Sporting News* names Gary the 1975 Rookie of the Year.

1977 —Gary hits three home runs in a game against Pittsburgh.

1980 —Gary becomes the only Expo to ever win the Montreal Player-of-the-Year Award three times.

1981

July —Gary hits two home runs in the All-Star Game in Cleveland. He is named MVP.

Oct. —Gary hits safely in all 10 games of the divisional and championship series, batting .429.

1982

July —Fans across the country give Gary 2,785,407 votes to lead the All-Star balloting.

Aug.—Gary gets his 1,000th major league hit off Bob Walk of the Atlanta Braves.

1983 —Gary is named to the All-Star Team for the sixth time and third as a starter.

ABOUT THE AUTHOR

Ray Buck is a sportswriter for the *Houston Post*. He has covered four World Series, six Super Bowls and three Wild West rodeos inside the Astrodome.

He is the author of five other books. *Dave Parker: The Cobra Swirl, Carlton Fisk: The Catcher Who Changed "Sox," Pete Rose: "Charlie Hustle,"* and *Danny White: The Kicking Quarterback* are also part of the Sports Star series. Ray's other book, *He Ain't No Bum* illustrates the cowboy philosophy and unique coaching ideals of New Orleans Saints Coach Bum Phillips.

Mr. Buck formerly covered the Cincinnati Reds and had the pleasure to watch Gary Carter 12 times a year. "We're lucky," says Mr Buck. "Gary Carter plays for the Montreal Expos but he acts like he belongs to the fans."